HOPE BEYOND PANDEMIC

BRUCE G. EPPERLY

Energion Publications
Gonzalez, Florida
2020

ISBN: 978-1-63199-529-3
eISBN: 978-1-63199-530-9
Library of Congress Control Number:

Energion Publications
PO Box 841
Gonzalez, FL 32560

https://energion.com
pubs@energion.com

TABLE OF CONTENTS

DISCERNING A WAY WHERE THERE IS NO WAY

We see in a mirror, dimly, but then we will see face to face. Now I know in part; then I will know fully even as I have been fully known. Now faith, hope, and love abide, these three; but the greatest of these is love. (1 Corinthians 13:12-13)

This afternoon as I look out my study window at the woods beyond our house, the world I see is filled with beauty. The Cape Cod sky is blue and the day is sunny. Later, after a day of writing and homeschooling, I plan to take a long walk with my grandchildren and our Golden Doodle on an empty beach near my home. On this glorious Cape Cod afternoon, for a few minutes, I can live in denial of the world around me. It is almost impossible to believe that as individuals and as a nation, virtually everything we are doing this Spring and into the Summer revolves around the Coronavirus pandemic. A virus, invisible to the naked eye, has shut down first world nations, shuttered restaurants and schools, and halted national and local economies. While politicians promise America's reopening and a resurgence of the economy, most of us recognize that life will never be the same again. I yearn to get back to normal, to the way things were on Ash Wednesday or New Year's Day. I dream of going to dinner and movie with my wife, museums and ball games with my grandchildren, shaking hands and embracing friends at church, potluck dinners, and in-person classes and study groups. I look forward to walking on the beach or my neighborhood without my face mask and in the company of good friends. Deep down, I know that there is no turning back, no return to the normal we once took for granted and the future we planned for ourselves, our families, and our congregations.

As we journey through the wilderness of pandemic eyes fixed on far horizons of hope, there is no clear road map ahead and no bright star guiding us to the promised land. The new normal for which we pray will be quite different than what we experienced in the weeks before mid-March 2020 when many of us closed our congregation's doors, suspended hospital and home visitation, and moved to online worship and programming. We are in the middle of an "apocalypse," the collapse of the old order and the end of business as usual.

The times are apocalyptic, but not as the feckless Second Coming preachers proclaim. There will be no divine rescue operation, separating the sheep and the goats, and providing escape for those who presume themselves among the saved. God will not deliver North America from the impact of the Coronavirus. The apocalypse we are going through is catastrophic, especially among the poor and vulnerable. There is no going back in time for a do over or reclaiming what has been destroyed. Still, we hope for a better tomorrow and some of us pray that within the destruction we are experiencing, seeds of transformation and global healing will emerge, like new growth following a forest fire. But there is no guarantee that many of the institutions and traditions that have defined our lives will survive.

As I ponder the meaning of these apocalyptic times, I believe the apocalypse we are going through is not a divinely planned catastrophe or judgment on the sins of the nation, but a "revealing" of where we stand in relationship to God, one another, and the planet. This revealing challenging our previously-held beliefs about our personal and global future can lead to repentance and transformed values if we discern the deeper challenges embedded in this time of personal, national, and global upheaval.

As I reflect on the future of our planet, nation, communities, and congregations, I feel much like Dante, who begins Canto One of *The Divine Comedy* with the confession, "In the middle of the journey of our life I came to myself within a dark wood where the straight way was lost." Right now, the way ahead is dark and uncertain with few social and political guideposts. Yet, as I write these words, we are in the middle of Easter season with Pentecost on the horizon. We can identify with the amazement of the woman who come desperate to Jesus' tomb, asking one another, "Who will roll away the stone for us from the entrance of the tomb?" and then discover that the tomb is empty and Christ is risen (Mark 16:3). We can yearn for the spiritual resuscitation and empowerment that emerged when Jesus' followers, anxiously sheltering in place in an upper room, suddenly experienced the Risen Jesus, promising peace, breathing on them, filling them with God's Spirit, enabling them to exhale once more, and then inspiring them to go out into the streets with good news of Life conquering death. We can also feel the amazement of the women and men, worshipping together behind closed doors, when the Holy Spirit bursts through and propels them out into the world with a message of spiritual transformation (Acts 2:1-13). A way was made when they had perceived no way forward. Like Jesus' first followers, we need spiritual resuscitation. We need to breathe in God's wisdom to find our bearings and discern our path forward.

These days, many of us feel like persons diagnosed with treatable, life-threatening diseases and in the middle of a cycle of chemotherapy or another treatment protocol. We yearn for recovery. We know the treatment will be difficult and painful and the outcome uncertain. In such desperate yet hopeful moments, we plead with Leo Tolstoy's Ivan Ilych, "I want to live!" Echoing back to us, as it did to Ilych, comes a question, "Do I want to live as I did before?" We know that in important ways we will never be the same after recovery. We also know that threats we face present us with possibilities for change. What new realities will we embrace? Will we hide away in fear, clinging to the way things were? Or will we go forth with hope, guided by inner wisdom of apocalypse, the divine revelings that lure us toward new horizons?

"Do we want to live as before?" In the wake of the stripping of national pretense and the threat of social collapse, how then shall we live — not just today but if, and when, we reach the promised land of vaccines and cures, and economic and congregational recovery? Will our experience of pandemic compel us to look at ourselves and our institutions in new ways? Will it help us unmask falsehoods to discover the truth about ourselves and our nation, or will we go back to the old ways as if nothing happened, content with our recovery while others remain mired in poverty and injustice? These are the questions that challenge me as a spiritual leader, writer, parent, grandparent, and citizen of a nation whose myth of progress and sense of exceptionalism has been shattered. We want, as commercials tell us, for life to go back to normal and political leaders promise a return to normalcy, if we can just get back to beaches, restaurants, and movie theaters, and pry open the economy.

Deep down, we know that after this crisis subsides, we may never get back to normal, at least the normal for which we had planned before March 2020. For those attuned to the signs of the times, the Coronavirus pandemic reveals other pandemics on the way, including one of our own making, global climate change. The pandemic also reveals the reality that what we once described as normal excluded and marginalized many of our siblings from the "good life" and put the planetary wellbeing at risk.

Despite our desire to turn back the clock, there is only one way for those of us who seek to follow the way of Jesus — forward toward a "new heaven and a new earth." We need to forge a new future, inspired by new visions of ourselves, our congregations, our national priorities, and our planet. We need healing and transformation of our hearts, minds, and relationships. We need to be prophets of a new era, acting on what has been revealed to us about ourselves and our nation.

Today, we are in the middle of a dark wood with no clear way forward. Yet, in the darkest night, the eye begins to glimpse the horizon, the glimmer of lights, and the outlines of paths in the wilderness. Plunged into the world of masks, physical distancing, sheltering in place except for my beach walk, and weekly home food and liquor deliveries, I felt the call to look beyond the pandemic, trying to imagine the first steps into an uncertain future. As the pandemic was emerging, I sought to find ways to remain faithful in a world turned upside down, and now I need to find an equally hopeful vision to inspire me as a spiritual leader, husband, and grandparent.[1]

As a middle class North American of European descent, privileged in many ways, I know my limits theologically, spiritually, and experientially. The pandemic has not given me a God's eye view and my perspective has been shaped by my social, ethnic, religious, and economic location as well as my nation of origin and spiritual commitments. I have food on my table and, for the moment, a salary to compensate for my pastoral telecommuting. I have the freedom and ability to distance myself from my neighbors and practice proper hygiene, unlike those in impoverished urban neighborhoods, refugee camps, and USA detention camps on our borderlands. I can work from home unlike farm workers and industrial workers being forced to go back to work in meat packing facilities under the threat of losing jobs and unemployment insurance.

Recognizing my limitations and the possibility of many alternative paths forward, I have sought the guidance of persons with other perspectives, religious commitments, and ethnic backgrounds as I attempt to discern a path ahead beyond the pandemic in a way that will inspire hopeful agency, most particularly among persons within the Christian community and those for whom the values of Jesus and the future of congregational life are of existential importance. I have also sought to listen to marginalized voices and communities that are now being hit, and will be continue to be hit, hardest by the pandemic as a result of age, risk factors, employment necessities, ethnicity, economics, and citizenship status. As a follower of Jesus, I must, nevertheless visualize and humbly work toward

---

1   Bruce Epperly, *Faith in a Time of Pandemic* (Gonzalez, FL: Energion Publications, 2020).

new life during and beyond the pandemic and imagine myself as a companion and midwife of God's realm on earth as it is in heaven.

This text reflects my prayerful reflections and spiritual practices as a pastor and theologian looking toward life beyond the pandemic. It is a "work in process," not only because I am a process theologian but because it is incomplete and fallible, subject to amendment, and hopefully will be joined by other visionaries — whose work will be more concrete and comprehensive — in articulating a new world whose imaginative reflections will supplement and move forward beyond my own. Like Paul, I look into a mirror dimly, hoping for greater illumination, and hoping for a new and better day, but fearing that things may get worse before they get better!

And so, with awe and amazement, fear and trembling, and knowing my limitations, I begin this humble and fallible reflection on hope beyond the pandemic. I pray for guidance and courage to be a companion in God's healing of the nation and planet. And so, as I consider the personal and social virtues essential for healing beyond the pandemic, I chart my course with the words of John Henry Cardinal Newman:

> Lead kindly light
> Amid the encircling gloom.
> The far shore I do not ask to see
> Just one step enough for me.

≈ ≈ ≈

A TIMELY WORD
WITHIN THE PANDEMIC, WE PROTEST

As this book went to press, the world was rocked by the brutal murder of George Floyd at the hands of those whose calling is to protect and serve. The death of George Floyd unmasked in graphic detail the American illusion of liberty and justice for all and the reality of systemic racism which has been exacerbated in this time of pandemic. In the spirit of the Hebraic prophets and Jesus of Nazareth, protest is the only appropriate response for people of faith. We need prophetic healing in our nation, but this will only come after we repent America's original sin of racism and genocide; materialism and economic idolatry, willing to sacrifice the vulnerable for financial and political gain; and environmental destruction putting at risk the non-human world, the wellbeing of our children and grandchildren and disproportionately persons of color and economic vulnerability.

Hope beyond pandemic must have at its heart an affirmation of diversity, a commitment to anti-racism, love of the earth, and preferential care for the most vulnerable. The moral arc bends long but hope comes when we push the moral and spiritual arcs forward as God's companions, God's hands and feet, in healing the earth. We protest and pray, knowing that God's vision of Shalom is the ultimate source of hope for persons and nations.

PRAYING FOR HEALING BEYOND PANDEMIC

Healing God, lead and guide us in this time of crisis and as we imagine a world beyond pandemic. Give us wisdom and compassion for the living of these days. Amen.

CHAPTER ONE

REPENTANCE

Suddenly the fingers of a human hand appeared and wrote on the plaster of the wall, near the lampstand in the royal palace. The king watched the hand as it wrote... This is the inscription that was written: MENE, MENE, TEKEL, PARSIN... "Here is what these words mean [Daniel said]: *Mene*: God has numbered the days of your reign and brought it to an end. *Tekel*: You have been weighed on the scales and found wanting. *Peres*: Your kingdom is divided and given to the Medes and Persians." (Daniel 5:5, 25-27)

Now after John was arrested, Jesus came to Galilee, proclaiming the good news of God, and saying, "The time is fulfilled, and the kingdom of God has come near; repent, and believe in the good news." (Mark 1:14-15)

Each moment is an opportunity for spiritual and moral transformation. Each moment brings divine revelings that call us forward toward new visions of ourselves and the world. The apostle Paul proclaims, "now is the day of salvation." (2 Corinthians 6:2) Deep down within even the most challenging moments of life, God is moving and calling us toward healing and wholeness as individuals and communities. The moral and spiritual arcs of history are not suspended during times of crisis and pandemic. In fact, I believe the arcs of healing and transformation accelerate as choices of life and death present themselves puncturing our illusions and sense of immunity from life's crises.

God's vision emerges most clearly when we abandon our own self-sufficiency and pride and awaken to healing movements of grace. We surely need grace in this time of pandemic. But our ability to experience God's offer of new creation relates to our willingness to repent and change our ways. No longer content with the ways of death, despite their apparent economic, political, and personal benefits, we realize that there is something more to life than power and prestige. We discover the importance of relationships, spirituality and community, and move from pride and passivity to repentance and agency.

THE WRITING ON THE WALL

As I write this morning, the fossil fuel industry is on the verge of temporary collapse with corporations paying for their crude oil to go to refineries. The much-vaunted USA medical system has been found unable to provide resources to test and treat. Lacking federal leadership and competence, states vie with one another and the federal government, often in clandestine ways, to secure face masks and ventilators. Nation first ideologies have been exposed as morally bankrupt and hazardous to our national and planetary health. Farm workers, truck drivers, nurses, physicians, and checkout clerks are labeled as "essential" and have been described as "heroes" while hedge fund investors and CEOs have been relegated to irrelevance in our quest for personal and national wellbeing. Though politicians vie with one another in science denial and billionaires and protesters embrace death for the sake of economic gain, the handwriting is on the wall. The values and practices that led to inadequate responses to the pandemic cannot save us in a time of pandemic. Nor will they provide respite from an even larger crisis to come, global climate change, for which there is no cure or vaccine except a transformation of values.

Celebrating the greatness of their high and mighty leader, Belshazzar and his court were confronted by the writing on the wall and discover that the nation was on the verge of collapse both internally and externally. The Babylonian kingdom had been so sure of its exceptionalism that it failed to see that its power and prestige were built on the shifting sands of injustice, violence, and oppression. The nation's leadership and social structures were weighed in the balance and found bereft of vision and morality. It appears that the American way is suffering the same fate, having built its house on the sands of materialism, consumption, income inequality, individualism, environmental destruction, and nation first ideology.

Though it has been a long time coming, the weakness of our system and the moral and spiritual bankruptcy of our values, often masqueraded as religious values by the court preachers, has been unmasked. The American Empire is collapsing before our eyes, hastened by the pandemic, and the unwillingness of the nation's leaders to repent our nation's misplaced values and priorities. Our illusions have been revealed by the pandemic, and we are presented with the opportunity to seek healing or continue in the ways of death. We pray that out of the collapse of the American empire, the Empire of Good will be born.

THE HEALING POWER OF DISILLUSIONMENT

These days many of us our depressed and disillusioned. Speaking as a citizen of the USA, our assumptions about our nation's health care system and economics have been shattered as we face the harsh realities of a global pandemic. In our opulence and convenience, we could not imagine disruptions to our food chain. We want to deny the daily death tolls and the ineptitude and indifference of our national leaders. Yet, denial will lead to death. Holding onto illusions will lead to passivity. Stripped of our illusions, we may discover, in the words of William Blake, that the doors of perception are cleansed and we can see the tragic beauty of life along with the paths of life and death stretching before us, and then be inspired to become agents of healing and hope. In the spirit of activist Angela Davis, we may assert:

> I am no longer accepting the things I cannot change.
> I am changing the things I cannot accept.

Recently I "crowdsourced" among my Facebook friends and an online theological reflection group I lead during this time of pandemic, made up of members of South Congregational Church and the wider community. I asked my companions to reflect on their assumptions and illusions that had been challenged as a result of the COVID-19 pandemic. The responses of these thoughtful and privileged North Americans and citizens of Great Britain were honest and sobering, yet within the disillusionment may be divine revelation as we look toward hopeful transformation beyond pandemic. They found the following assumptions no longer tenable:

- It can't happen here
- Our exceptionalism as a nation
- The superiority of our health care system
- White, powerful, and wealthy exceptionalism
- My privilege can protect me
- Superpowers can beat this
- Science can beat this
- Individualism is healthy
- Consumerism is good for everyone
- USA is #1
- That Americans really care about democracy and the checks and balances in government
- We are strong enough to fix this; a quick fix is on the way
- We will get back to normal and soon
- Economic issues are more important than personal issues
- I'll have enough financial security for retirement
- I will have health care and that the hospital will treat me
- I'll never lose my job
- The American economy is indestructible
- The national government will protect and serve
- Our leaders know what they're doing and care about us
- I'll have toilet paper

My theological and social media companions are clear that the handwriting is on the wall and that the United States' political and economic leadership — indeed the vaunted American way of life

— has been weighed in the balances and has been found wanting in both compassion and competence.

One online companion's response provided a ray of hope as she confessed "I used to think people were greedy. Now I'm realizing that we are also generous and willing to sacrifice to help others." Painful as it may be, examining our assumptions is essential to repentance, recognizing the handwriting on the wall, confessing our complicity in the evils we deplore, and turning our lives and nation around.

THE DANGER OF DENIAL AND GASLIGHTING

The Coronavirus pandemic has inspired truth telling, scientific analysis, and creative disillusionment. The apocalypse has revealed the necessity for personal and global transformation. Sadly, it has also led to willful disinformation in the news and social media and mixed messages from the highest levels of government. Science denial among conservative Christians has directly or indirectly contributed to the spread of the Coronavirus. Religious leaders have pitted faith against science, repeating the losing battles their predecessors fought against Galileo and Darwin. Pastors have held church services falsely assuming God would protect their congregations from the contagion. Testing their assumption that they are God's chosen, they believe that Jesus is their vaccine and that they don't need to pay attention to scientific data! Grounded in their desire to pander to their conservative Christian base, politicians have denied scientific evidence regarding the spread of the Coronavirus. They have challenged scientific fact to promote their economic agendas, putting low income workers at greatest risk. Billionaires, safely quarantined in penthouses and estates, advocate for opening the economy regardless of the consequence for the common good and their most economically vulnerable employees, many of whom are persons of color. Politicians rewrite history, denying any culpability and scapegoating anyone who challenges the wisdom of their political decision-making.

Reflecting on what he perceives to be the growing scientific and intellectual dishonesty of political, business, and religious leaders, film maker Julio Vincent Gambuto warns us that we are on the verge of the most breathtaking gaslighting operation in history. Gaslighting, the attempt to redefine reality so that we no longer believe what we have seen and heard, is one of the primary marketing and intellectual tools of the powers and principalities. According to Gambuto, "What is about to be unleashed on American society will be the greatest campaign ever created to get you to feel normal again. It will come from brands, it will come from government, it will even come from each other, and it will come from the left and from the right. We will do anything, spend anything, believe anything, just so we can take away how horribly uncomfortable all of this feels."

Now, there are many benefits of returning to normalcy. We want to get together with friends, go to worship services in our churches, go out to dinner and the movies, take our children to the park for sports activities, and go on holiday again. We want to shop without wearing masks or gloves or scour the aisles in search of toilet paper and disinfectant. As I write, I have several speaking engagements that are pending until we get the "all clear." I want to get back on the road to see North America and share good news in person. But "normal" also includes pollution, climate change, income inequality, rights without responsibilities, toddlers in borderland concentration camps, systemic racism, and rampant consumerism. In family life, normal often means extended time away from home and on the run parenting. It also means the death-dealing policies of politicians quietly dismantling environmental protection regulations while we are focusing on the Coronavirus.

The Coronavirus has questioned our previously held values and assumptions about the American way of life. Our desire to explore alternative visions of politics, health care, economics, and political involvement will endanger the status quo, economic privilege, and our own security. Still, according to Gambuto:

What the trauma has shown us, though, cannot be un-seen. A carless Los Angeles has clear blue skies as pollution has simply stopped. In a quiet New York, you canhear the birds chirp in the middle of Madison Avenue. Coyotes have been spotted on the Golden Gate Bridge. These are the postcard images of what the world might be like if we could find a way to have a less deadly daily effect on the planet. What's not fit for a postcard are the other scenes we have witnessed: a health care system that cannot provide basic protective equipment for its frontline; small businesses — and very large ones — that do not have enough cash to pay their rent or workers, sending over 16 million people to seek unemployment benefits [at the time of this writing]; a government that has so severely damaged the credibility of our media that 300 million people don't know who to listen to for basic facts that can save their lives.[2]

Faithfulness requires repentance, and repentance requires us to see life as it is without dishonesty or disinformation. Honest recognition of our intentional and unintentional complicity with the pathways of environmental, economic, and spiritual death is the foundation of the transformational healing required for persons and institutions.

PROPHETIC FACT CHECKING.

As a child raised in an evangelical Christian church, I often attended revival meetings and regularly watched Billy Graham's "Hour of Decision" on television. A staple of revival Christianity was the hymn "Just as I Am" often repeated several times during the service as a call to repentance, an opportunity to come to Jesus. I can still repeat the words of Charlotte Elliott's hymn by heart, although I now understand them quite differently than I did as a child.

2   Julio Vincent Gambuto, "Prepare for the Ultimate Gaslighting."
— https://forge.medium.com/prepare-for-the-ultimate-gaslighting-6a8ce3f0a0e0

Just as I am — without one plea,
But that Thy blood was shed for me,
And that Thou bid'st me come to Thee,
—O Lamb of God, I come!...

Just as I am — though toss'd about
With many a conflict, many a doubt,
Fightings and fears within, without,
—O Lamb of God, I come!

Just as I am — poor, wretched, blind;
Sight, riches, healing of the mind,
Yea, all I need, in Thee to find,
—O Lamb of God, I come!

Now more than ever I can identify with these words as they express the reality of personal and institutional sinfulness, the necessity of complete honesty and self-awareness in facing the Coronavirus, and the unceasing and life-transforming grace of God that heals our hearts and minds and calls us to a life of compassionate service. "Just as I Am" is a call to mindfulness and self-examination, enabling us to see ourselves and our nation without filter, self-justification or political posturing and scapegoating, and in that honesty, repent, accept God's grace, and become agents of justice and mercy.

In a way I did not understand as a child — and few evangelicals understand today — this hymn is prophetic in spirit. At the heart of the prophetic message, championed over twenty-five hundred years ago by Amos, Hosea, Micah, Isaiah, and Jeremiah was the quest to see the "signs of the times" through the lens of God's vision of Shalom. The prophets were committed to unvarnished honesty about themselves and their nation. In contrast to today's political leaders who trade on prevarication, dissembling, and historical revisionism, the prophets confronted their nation with theological Lysol, cleansing heart and mind, of disingenuousness, dishonesty, and deviltry. With Senator Daniel Patrick Moynihan, they recognized that they — and their fellow citizens — were entitled to their own opinions but not their own facts!

The greatest harm political prevarication and disinformation creates in times of crisis is lack of trust which leads to citizens' unwillingness to sacrifice for the wellbeing of one's neighbors and the nation's wellbeing. The greatest harm religious dishonesty can create, in the joining of congregational and political realms, is the assumption that our viewpoints reflect God's biases and that an attack on our values and way of life is an attack on God. The words of the prophets may be written on subway walls and, also, in medical counsel regarding testing, sheltering in place, and the trajectory of a pandemic. For those who humbly seek the truth, divine wisdom and apocalyptic is found in medical research labs as well as in sanctuaries and meditation halls.

The Hebraic prophets and their descendants Jesus and John the Baptist recognized that healing of the spirit, like healing of the body, begins with an accurate assessment of our personal and political wellbeing. Without facts, authentic transformation is impossible. Trading in falsehood, magical thinking, and dishonesty, whether in our professional and personal lives, or from a pulpit or press conference from the White House, disempowers those around us, destroys trust, and deadens the spirit. Faithfulness requires facts. Today's prophets demand accuracy in relationship to economic equality, climate change, and progress of the Coronavirus. The biblical tradition claims that all-loving and all-knowing God has a bias and so do God's prophets, and the articulation of God's vision is grounded in a clear sense of "what's going on," to quote soul singer Marvin Gaye. As one of my Georgetown University colleagues, physician Edmund Pellegrino asserted, ethics — whether medical or prophetic — requires three questions:

- What is the situation?
- What can I do?
- What ought I to do?

These three questions apply equally to congregational life and political decision-making.

Prophetic factuality, like an accurate medical diagnosis, provides the foundation for the healing we need spiritually, economically, relationally, and politically. Recognizing where we are — just as we are "without one plea" — opens the door to God's call, "now is the day of transformation." In that "come to Jesus moment," falsehood gives way to truth, sickness to healing, and passivity to agency. Wounded healers, we now become prophetic healers, inspired by the interplay of self-awareness, confession, humility, grace, and empowerment. As prophetic healers, we challenge the forces of destruction, even in ourselves, as a prelude to healing, reconciliation, and transformation. Discerning God's horizons of hope requires faith and it also requires realism and challenge. We must pass through the valley of disillusionment and confession — and perhaps despair and grief — to experience the new horizons of possibility for ourselves and our nation

HOPEFUL ACTIVISM

John the Baptist came to the Jordan River, preaching a message of repentance that unmasked his hearers' illusions, ethnic and religious assumptions, and sense of privilege and superiority (Matthew 3:1-12 and Luke 31-14). Utterly disillusioned yet freed from the burden of self-righteousness and self-justification, those whom the Baptist described as a "brood of vipers," plead for guideposts to personal transformation. "What should we do?" to be part of God's realm of Shalom, they asked. John's advice was straightforward, "Bear fruit worthy of repentance." Change your priorities and change your lives. His advice to his listeners, many of whom were the economic and military elite, was political as well as personal: if you want to be part of God's Shalom, change your ways, be honest in your business dealings, share with the poor, practice nonviolence and honesty in enforcing the law, tell the truth. God's realm involves clearing the detritus of dishonesty and injustice as a prelude to transformation. "Now is the time to choose life for yourself, your nation, and the planet," counsel — or dare we say, demand — prophets then and now as they seek healing within and the pandemic.

Our fruits of repentance must in terms of ethics involve a commitment to factuality and honesty. Look deeply at your sources of information. What and whom do they privilege? What do they omit? Whose stories do they report? Whose lives do they neglect? Look for bias in the media and your own perspective that prevent you from seeing life as it is. Make a commitment to a politics of truth and factuality, challenging the assumptions of political and religious leaders when they bend the truth to support their agenda. This even applies to politicians and leaders we support. Tell the truth with compassion and require it of your political leaders.

SPIRITUALITY BEYOND PANDEMIC

The times call for self-examination and mindful living to liberate us from our illusions and the powers of death and destruction. In this practice, a version of Ignatius of Loyola's Examen, take time regularly for the following prophetic mindfulness practice.

- Begin with stillness, breathing deeply centering yourself in God's grace.
- Recognize any anxiety, fear, and stress that emerges and place it in God's care.
- Give thanks for God's love manifest in your life, relationships, and the world.
- Pause again with a few deep breaths.
- Reflect on your current spiritual values. Where are you complicit with the powers of evil and destruction? Where have you turned from God's vision for yourself and the world? Where are your biases, experiences, and social location (economics, ethnicity, education, etc.) preventing you from seeing life as it is for the most vulnerable?
- Pray for a prophetic healing of your mind and spirit.

– Make a commitment to honesty, factuality, and justice-seeking
– Pray for guidance in the day ahead.
– Trust God with your future and with the way ahead as you seek a new way of life.

In response to the prophetic call to repent and turn from the ways of death, I conclude with another revival hymn from my childhood, John Newton's "Amazing Grace:

Amazing grace,
How sweet the sound,
That saved a wretch like me,
I once was lost but now I'm found,
Was blind but now I see.

'Twas grace that taught my heart to fear
and grace my fears relieved.
How precious did that grace appear
The hour I first believed.

PRAYING FOR HEALING BEYOND THE PANDEMIC

God of Love and Challenge, convict us of our complicity with the evils we deplore. Challenge our complacency. Open our hearts and senses to your pain at the world's suffering and inspire us to join you in the healing of the world. Amen.

CHAPTER TWO

GRATITUDE

Rejoice in the Lord always; again I will say, Rejoice. Let your gentleness be known to everyone. The Lord is near. Do not worry about anything, but in everything by prayer and supplication with thanksgiving let your requests be made known to God. And the peace of God, which surpasses all understanding, will guard your hearts and your minds in Christ Jesus. (Philippians 4:4-7)

Throughout this time of pandemic, I chose to begin my day with two brief affirmations: "This is the day that the Lord has made, let me rejoice and be glad in it" (Psalm 118, AP) and "I thank you God for waking me up today." These prayers remind me that despite the challenges I face and the realities of disease and death, each day is an adventure filled with possibilities for spiritual and intellectual growth, creativity, love, and mission. These affirmations inspire me to agency and repentance, and to commit myself to do something beautiful for God as I challenge what others believe cannot be changed and open my heart to people who are forgotten and marginalized. They remind me that in the dark wood, God makes a way when we perceive no way.

Gratitude has become the order of the day in the media and on our doorsteps. We hear words of thanks to health care workers on television commercials and from newscasters. Banners are raised in my neighborhood, thanking physicians, nurses, and first responders. We profusely thank persons who deliver our groceries and work at the grocers. We acknowledge the "essential" work of farm workers, many of whom are undocumented residents, scientists and researchers, truckers, food packers, first responders, and letter carriers. For this moment in time, we are living in a world of gratitude. We are discovering that the real job creators are not

CEO's but hardworking laborers, tradespersons, dispatchers, and middle managers. The real job creators, the people who make the world go round, are ordinary people who trust our governmental and business leaders to tell them that it is safe to shop at the grocery store or go to work. It takes a village to raise a child. It also takes the support and commitment of a village to make a business prosper for the common good of its neighborhood.

Thanksgiving is the virtue of interconnectedness. When we are thankful, we remember that there is no such thing as a self-made person. Our successes are the result of the sacrifices and contributions of others — parents and grandparents, schoolteachers, pastors, Christian educators, farmers and industrial workers, military personnel, and so many others. I am writing these words with a sense of gratitude to my father Everett whose faithful ministry inspired my interest in theology, my professors who introduced me to rigorous and imaginative philosophical and theological thinking, my spiritual teachers who introduced me to meditation and contemplative prayer, the students I've taught, and the congregants I've pastored who inspired me intellectual excellence and spiritual integrity. I give thanks for my mother who loved me fiercely and whose prayers guided me in ways she could never imagine. I have been blessed to be born in the United States, the beneficiary of a good public education, a stable environment, and goods and services that ensured my health and wellbeing. I am the person I am today as a result of the love of my wife of over forty years Kate and a few spiritual friends who inspired me to settle for nothing less than excellence in my personal and professional life, writing, and spiritual endeavors. As the Southern African saying goes, "I am because we are."

GRATITUDE AS POLITICAL.

Thanksgiving as the virtue of interconnectedness is profoundly ethical and political. The Epistle of James proclaims, "faith by itself, if it has no works, is dead" (James 3:17). The same applies to gratitude. Our gratitude must not be gratuitous — words are cheap. Thanksgiving, like grace, must cost us something. Once again, the Epistle of James provides spiritual and ethical challenge if we restrict our thanksgiving merely to a banner, word, or greeting card.

> What good is it, my brothers and sisters, if you say you have faith, but do not have works? Can faith save you? If a brother or sister is naked and lacks daily food, and one of you says, "Go in peace; keep warm and eat your fill, and yet you do not supply their bodily needs, what is the good of that?" (James 3:14-16)

These words convict us when we are tempted to soothe our spirits with cheap thanksgiving. Many of the most essential workers today are employed in low pay, menial jobs, or lack job security or health care benefits. Consider the persons who pick and package our fruits and vegetables and work at our nursing homes, most earning less than $15 per hour, including many undocumented residents, who may pay taxes but receive none of the benefits given to other citizens. Reflect on the overworked and heartbroken farmer, hurt already by the tariff war with China and now having to plow their fields or dump milk because physical distancing has led to closing restaurants, bars, and theme parks. Remember the person receiving modest remuneration for delivering or packing your groceries, or checkout clerks, many of whom are not unionized or receive adequate health care benefits. Appreciation is valued but as the athlete, played by Cuba Gooding, Jr., in the film *Jerry Maguire* shouts, "Show me the money!"

Persons of faith know that money is not all-important, but they also recognize that just compensation is important as a reflection of our values. The ethics of gratitude challenge us to ensure that every worker receives fair and just compensation, adequate for providing housing, healthy food, entertainment, and a safe and secure environment. Having been blessed to be a blessing, our gratitude leads to ensuring health care and education as a right for every family. We need to extend our gratitude immediately to undocumented residents, who have been obeying the law and providing essential services in this time of pandemic, by a clear and straightforward path to citizenship along with a suspension of all deportation proceedings and ICE arrests except in the case for serious crimes. Gratitude to the children of undocumented workers, now teenagers who have spent virtually all their lives in the USA, demands that "dreamers" should receive immediate citizenship. Those who invoke the superficial shibboleth "family values" need to be reminded that the health of families depends on minimizing economic and personal stress and insecurity, especially related to unwarranted deportation and separation of parents and children. The stress of undocumented families would be reduced by long term legal security and health care. As we have discovered in this time of pandemic, at risk farmworkers, who work daily to put food on our tables, are a public health danger as well as at greater personal health risk as a result of their fear of going to a hospital and lack of health insurance. I believe that the words of the prophets, privileging the least of these and marginalized, ring out in protest to the injustices and brutality of our immigration policy.

> God has told you, O mortal, what is good; and what does
> the LORD require of you but to do justice, and to love kindness,
> and to walk humbly with your God? (Micah 6:8)

We have been given much. Our calling now is solidarity with the vulnerable and justice to the marginalized. In God's realm of Shalom, there is no "other." All that we do to the least of these is received by God to whom all hearts are open and all desires known. Every act of grateful generosity brings joy to God and adds to the beauty of God's experience and this good earth.

HOPEFUL ACTIVISM

Gratitude without works is gratuitous! Thanksgiving inspires us to political and social action. Prayerfully contact your state and local representatives urging them to support fair wages and health care insurance for essential workers, cessation of deportation for law abiding workers, and the expansion of benefits to undocumented workers who daily perform essential social tasks. Sheltering in place, you can donate financially to your food bank, safely cook and deliver a casserole to a shelter, where many of our working poor reside, and challenge your leaders to begin to look beyond the pandemic in providing wage increases, health care that persists regardless of employment situation, and inexpensive day care for the children of today's working poor as you advocate for higher wages for working Americans.

SPIRITUALITY IN A TIME OF PANDEMIC

Thanksgiving opens our hearts and minds and liberates us from unhealthy self-preoccupation. Thanksgiving awakens us to trust the enduring realities of Life and the Providence of God despite the threats we face. The grateful cannot moan "woe is me." The grateful delight in small acts of kindness and beauty and bring out the best in others. Let us give thanks for the bounties we have received as we remember the hymn penned by seventeenth century German pastor Martin Rinkart, who served God during a time of plague.

> Now thank we all our God,
> with heart and hands and voices,
> Who wondrous things has done,
> in Whom this world rejoices;
> Who from our mothers' arms
> has blessed us on our way
> With countless gifts of love,
> and still is ours today.

PRAYING FOR HEALING BEYOND THE PANDEMIC

Thank you for awakening me this morning to a day of possibility and action. Let me count my blessings and out of my blessings, let me bless the world. Amen.

CHAPTER THREE

COMMUNITY

If one member suffers, all suffer together with it; if one member is honored, all rejoice together with it. Now you are the body of Christ and individually members of it. (1 Corinthians 12:26-27)

Throughout this time of pandemic, we are told over and over that "we are all in this together." These words are intended to remind us that we are responsible for the wellbeing of our communities, that what we do shapes the health of vulnerable people, and that despite physical distancing we are spiritually, emotionally, and relationally connected. We have discovered that, in the intricate interdependence of life, wearing a mask in public and sheltering in place are acts of love, caring for our neighbor as we would care for ourselves!

Ecologists remind us that the statement "we are in this together" was true in November 2019 before any of us had heard of the Coronavirus and that this same statement will also be true after the virus subsides and we have discovered a vaccine and cure. The interdependence of life has been a central affirmation of process theologians for whom the whole universe inspires to create each moment of experience. A butterfly flapping its wings in Pacific Grove shapes the weather on Cape Cod. A random act of kindness to a weary stranger can transform several generations just as an errant sneeze can spread the Coronavirus. Choosing to remain seated on a bus can be a catalyst for civil rights legislation. Staying on your couch rather than mixing in crowds and wearing a mask when you go out can be a matter of life and death for persons you have never met as well as yourself. This profound interconnectedness has been at the heart of the environmental movement's recognition that our behaviors have an impact on the quality of air, water, and land in towns and villages distant from our homes.

The interdependence of life reminds us that there is no such thing as an isolated individual, community, state, or nation. The Coronavirus alerts us to the spiritual, moral, and political bankruptcy of nation-first, we can do it alone, ideologies. In fact, many now believe that the idolatry of national sovereignty, evident in the behavior of China as well the USA nation-first foreign and economic policies, has been a factor in the spread of the pandemic. Nation-first ideologies and political policies turn us inward, promoting national isolation, cutting off supplies of medical goods and scientific information. They inspire us to think that the problems of other nations can't touch us and thus leave us unprepared when pandemic strikes.

The affirmation "we are all in this together" challenges us to transcend national selfishness in favor of ensuring the wellbeing of humankind as part of our planetary loyalty. The pandemic has shown us that borders are permeable and walls cannot defend us against viruses. We must prize local governments and cultures and encourage people to act, eat, and shop locally. But without a global spirit, emphasis on our own kin ultimately puts at risk those whom we most love.

The ethics of interdependence challenges us to join local and global in responding to the pandemic. As followers of Jesus, we recognize that the rain falls and the sun shines not only on the "righteous" and the "unrighteous," but also on the British and the Iranian, the Russian and the Canadian, the Ugandan and the Australian, and the American and Chinese. God's love for the world embraces all creation. While some nations and locales may align themselves more fully with God's vision of Shalom, God affirms the uniqueness of each nation and its vocation as a companion in God's healing of the earth. God loves the child living without electricity and running water as much as God loves my own grandchildren with their laptops, snacks, video games, and art projects. God loves the fetus growing in the womb and God also loves the right whale baby, a new member of a species of the verge of extinction. Spiritual growth involves the mystic vision, translated into action, of God in all things and all things in God!

Recognizing the intricate fabric of relatedness, Martin Luther King affirmed: "For some strange reason I cannot be what I ought to be until you are what you ought to be. And you can never be what you ought to be until I am what I ought to be. That's the way the God's universe is made."[3]

Beyond the pandemic, our vocation is to continue living by the motto "we are all in this together" whether in terms of economics, politics, spirituality, ecology, or national sovereignty. Individualistic self-interest is no longer tenable in an interdependent world. As cells in the "body of Christ" (1 Corinthians 12:12-31), everyone matters. Justice seeking for all creation is imperative. The wellbeing of undocumented residents is necessary for our wellbeing, not just economically but spiritually. The experiences of a Sudanese family shape the spiritual temperature of the planet. If we neglect the wellbeing of the least of these, distancing ourselves from our human and non-human siblings, we will experience a famine of hearing the word of God (Amos 8). Our sanctuaries will become graveyards and not mouthpieces of the Holy Spirit. In contrast, when we hear God's voice in the vulnerable stranger in our neighborhood or across the globe, we are transported into a God-filled world where churches come alive as poets of God's Spirit, children dance and sing, elders rejoice in the beauty of the day, and all creation reveals the message of grace beyond pandemic.

HOPEFUL ACTIVISM

Mahatma Gandhi asserted that there is enough for everyone's need but not for everyone's greed. Simplicity of life among North Americans is essential for the survival of the majority — developing — world. Decluttering is more than just getting rid of unnecessary

---

3   Martin Luther King *A Knock at Midnight* (New York: Warner Books, 2000), 208.

possessions. It involves seeking first God's realm through solidarity, simplicity, and sacrifice.

As part of your commitment to the health of our planet, make a commitment, first, to examine your patterns of consumption. While recognizing the value of celebrations and healthy diets, consider where your consumerism threatens the overall wellbeing of the planet and its most vulnerable people. Learn to eat more simply, and lower on the food chain. Explore planting a garden at home, buying from local farmers, and going to locally sourced restaurants. When possible eat organic foods and cut your meat consumption to lessen your impact on the earth. We can't do everything, but we can do something to claim our agency as God's companions in healing the earth.

SPIRITUAL PRACTICES IN A TIME OF PANDEMIC.

Psalm 150:6 proclaims, "let everything that breathes praise God." Jesus breathes on his followers and says "Receive the Holy Spirit." (John 20:19-22) Breath is essential to life, and yet many of us are waiting to exhale in this time of pandemic. We need to take an "all clear" breath to remind us that God is with us, despite our anxieties and the limitations of sheltering in place. Breath reminds us that we are connected with all creation — with the child wanting to play outside in Wu Han, the pregnant woman in Ohio (the daughter of one of my wife's best friend from high school) rushed to the maternity ward in a time of pandemic, the adult children unable to visit their dying parent sequestered in the hospital, a defensive and insecure political leader bullying and bloviating, a first responder risking their lives for the safety of others.

In this spiritual practice, simply breathe deeply God's presence. Let every breath fill you with the Spirit. Let your breathing bring calm, enlivening your cells and soul. Feel each inhaled breath as a gift from the planet, connecting you with every creature, human and non-human. As you exhale, let your breathing be a prayer of healing connection with the earth and its creatures. Breathe out gratitude, compassion, and love as you remember the words of Edwin Hatch's hymn:

> Breathe on me breath of God,
> Fill me with life anew,
> That I may love what Thou would love,
> And do what Thou would do.

Praying for Healing Beyond Pandemic.

Holy one, awaken us to the intricate interdependence of life. Help us live by the words of the hymn:

> *"Blest be the tie that binds*
> *our hearts in Christian love*
> *The fellowship of kindred minds*
> *is like to that above."*

Amen.

Chapter Four

Compassion

As he came near and saw the city, he wept over it, saying,
"If you, even you, had only recognized on this day the things
that make for peace! But now they are hidden from your eyes.
(Luke 19:41-42)

The interdependence of life invites us to see God's face in the
faces of others. The Holy peeks out of every corner of the universe.
The patriarch Jacob awakens from dreaming of a ladder of angels,
proceeding from earth to heaven and back again, and exclaims,
"God was in this place and I did not know it." The spiritual lesson
of pandemic is that God is in every place and all persons, especially
the most vulnerable, are God's beloved children. This vision of a
God-filled universe transforms our hearts and our politics.

A saying suggests that the difference between ignorance and
apathy is "I don't know" and "I don't care." The pandemic has revealed our illusions of independence and ignorance. We know the
earth is on fire, not just with the current pandemic but in terms of
shortages in health care, medical supplies, and necessities for North
Americans, such as paper towels, hand sanitizer, and toilet paper.
We are tempted to turn away when, from our position of economic
privilege, we view photos of farmworkers working at low wages,
at risk, in grueling heat, with little sanitation. We want to hide
our eyes when we see news reports of refugee camps and third, or
majority, world nations in which people are forced to live alongside
each other unable to practice physical distancing, with shortages
in running water, disinfectants, and sanitary facilities. Our hearts
break when we hear of seniors dying in nursing homes, separated
from their families for hygiene reasons, and toddlers separated from

their parents to fulfill inhumane campaign promises. We do know, but will we care?

Jesus weeps over Jerusalem, mirroring the Parental Heart of the Universe, who feels our every longing, is touched by every tear, delights in every celebration, and weeps with our own tears as we see the rising death tolls. The Heart of the Universe mourns every death and protests every injustice and act of neglect. Imagine that — God weeps! God laments the death toll and God grieves our personal insensitivity and governmental inaction, often intentional, in response to the pain of the vulnerable.

The One who inspired prophets fuels our own prophetic critique of political ineptitude and indifference and calls us to align ourselves with God's own moral and spiritual arcs of history, challenging us to move from apathy to empathy and passivity to agency. The All Compassionate One inspires our own compassionate embrace of the pain of the world. Imagine that — God mourns and protests!

God is empathetic, not apathetic, and inspires by Divine Companionship our own empathy. God calls us to be like Jesus, to grow in "wisdom and stature." Stature enables us to embrace the pain of others while preserving our own spiritual integrity and centeredness. Wisdom enables us to look beyond self and national interest to long term and broad based solutions to the challenges we face. According to pioneering process-relational theologian, Bernard Loomer:

> By size I mean the stature of a person's soul, the range and depth of his love, his capacity for relationships. I mean the volume of life you can take into your being and still maintain your integrity and individuality, the intensity and variety of outlook you can entertain in the unity of your being without feeling defensive or insecure. I mean the strength of your spirit to encourage others to become freer in the development of their diversity and uniqueness.[4]

---

4   Harry James Cargas and Bernard Lee, (*Religious Experience and Process Theology.* Mahweh, NJ: PaulistPress. 1976), 70.

Whenever I am on retreat at a Benedictine monastery, I am inspired by the counsel, "Treat everyone as Christ." Christ is revealed in all his disguises whether in an overworked nurse or physician, a lonely senior adult, a bored child, a grandparent gasping for breath dying of COVID-19, and a politician more concerned with getting the economy going and scoring political points than providing for the lives of our most vulnerable citizens. As we go beyond the pandemic, we need to live by the words of Jesus:

> … for I was hungry and you gave me food, I was thirsty and you gave me something to drink, I was a stranger and you welcomed me, I was naked and you gave me clothing, I was sick and you took care of me, I was in prison and you visited me…Truly I tell you, just as you did it to one of the least of these who are members of my family, you did to me. (Matthew 25:35-36, 40)

I believe that we are called not only to see with God's eyes but also be Christ's hands, feet, and heart. Early Christian theologians, such as Irenaeus and Athanasius, asserted that God became human so that we might become divine. While none of us can claim to be Christ or be fully aligned with Christ's vision, we can see Christ in the least of these and be Christ to the least of these. Opening to God's moment by moment vision, we can embody God's love, doing something beautiful and healing in each encounter. In my own quest to be Christlike, one of my personal affirmations is "I bless everyone I meet" and though I often fail to live up to this, it is my relational polestar. God wants us to be, as Luther says, little Christs sharing the grace God has bestowed on us with our neighbor. God also invites us to embody the spirit of the Bodhisattva, who refuses solitary enlightenment to bring enlightenment and healing to the world.

A POLITICS OF COMPASSION.

The times call for compassion, most particularly a politics of compassion. Individual compassion is not enough. We need structures of compassion that prioritize the wellbeing of the most vulnerable, those who bear the brunt of the pandemic, and those who have experienced a lifetime of small and large injustices based on race, ethnicity, sexuality, and health condition. We have seen the pandemic's impact on the African American community and indigenous people, already the victims of slavery and genocide. Some form of political repentance is mandated today, not just confessions of our social and political sins, but appropriate restoration and reparation on a community basis. Georgetown University, where I served as Protestant Chaplain and taught theology and medicine for two decades, now gives preferential admission to the descendants of slaves who were sold to fund the university. A politics of compassion proclaims that we are not whole as a nation until everyone is given the opportunity to become whole. Out of the ashes of pandemic, we may discover that everyone is essential to the wellbeing of our communities and that truly no one — and no group — can be left behind in the quest for a just and sustainable economic system.

HOPEFUL ACTIVISM

Active faith beyond pandemic challenges us to do our homework. Facts matter, and key to ethical and just advocacy is knowing the facts about economic, legal, and environmental injustice, immigration, childhood poverty, domestic violence, white racism, and global climate change. I must caution you that moving from ignorance to information and apathy to empathy will be painful, and you need to spiritually prepare for what you discover. You also need to embrace your emotions, your tears and anger as reflecting God's Open Heart. For your own wellbeing and sense of agency it is also essential to find persons who share your commitments to justice both for personal support and political advocacy.

While you're on the couch, you can pick up the phone! Our representatives need to hear that we cannot go back to pre-pandemic injustice and ignorance. Tell your representatives that they need to act on behalf of vulnerable persons, victims of injustice, and immigrants.

We must alert them to our belief that undocumented residents and families separated from one another on our borderlands are God's children, bearing the image of God and must be treated justly. The personal is the political and justice and compassion deferred is an indictment against our nation and an offense to God.

SPIRITUAL PRACTICES BEYOND PANDEMIC

In this exercise, we begin with silence as a reflection of our commitment to the practice of contemplative prayer. Contemplative prayer, whether meditation, breath prayer, silence, or chanting, awakens us to God's presence in our lives, deepens our sense of peace, and brings a sense of calm to our activism. From a quiet center, we are strengthened for the difficult journey ahead, personally and politically.

In a quiet and comfortable place, breathe deeply and slowly. As you breathe, begin to visualize your connection to the world around you. Visualize the varieties of humankind, ethnically, religiously, economically, nationally, and so forth. Experience your unity with all creation and humankind. See the faces of diverse humanity, looking for Christ in each face. Let your imagination uncover the holiness of each person as God's beloved child. Commit yourself to seeing Christ and being Christ to everyone you meet, most especially the forgotten, vulnerable, and marginalized. In stillness, we can pray with the Celtic sages,

> Be thou my Vision, O Lord of my heart...
> Be thou my Wisdom, and thou my true Word,
> I ever with the and Thou with me, Lord.

PRAYING FOR HEALING BEYOND THE PANDEMIC

Open my heart, Loving Companion, to your presence in every life. Open my arms to safely hug and hands to share. Let love guide my words and meditations, and let all creation find peace. Amen.

CHAPTER FIVE

JUSTICE

Let justice roll down like waters, and righteousness like an ever-flowing stream. (Amos 5:24)

The Coronavirus has revealed in stark details the realities of injustice in America. Economic and judicial disparity existed long before the pandemic and it is likely that the pandemic will exacerbate inequalities that deaden the spirit and jeopardize the health of millions of Americans. Indeed, the pandemic has been apocalyptic in its revelation of the fragility, inequity, and ecological devastation beneath our apparent economic prosperity. In my own state, hospitalization records indicate that there are higher rates of Coronavirus in communities with "dirty air," each of which has a high percentage of minority, low-income residents, and accordingly high rates of asthma and other environmentally-related respiratory diseases.

During the time of pandemic, persons of color are at greater risk than the overall population as a result of health factors such as hypertension, diabetes, and obesity and accessibility to health care. These risks have been accentuated due to employment and housing that prevents telecommuting, sheltering in place, and the physical separation, all of which are available to professional workers living in suburban neighborhoods. African Americans, Latinos, and immigrants are at the front lines of nursing home care, farm work, food packing, grocery sales, and food distribution. Unlike salaried employees, they have few health benefits and often receive modest, if any, sick leave. In most non-union workplaces, no work means no pay and the greater likelihood that persons experiencing COVID-19 and other respiratory illnesses will show up for work simply to feed their families. This same reality also applies to low income European Americans, lacking education and training, and the USA's first peoples, many of whom lack the medical resources and economic infrastructure, especially on reservations, available to more affluent communities.

Economists anticipate that the long-term negative economic impact of the Coronavirus will be greater among persons of color, non-union employees, and unskilled workers of all races. As I write in early May 2020, workers are being forced to work at "essential" meat packing factories, even though they are at greater risk of COVID-19 due to the virtual impossibility of physical distancing. Not going to work may mean loss of unemployment benefits, so the risk is necessary in the eyes of family breadwinners. To compound the injustice attending the pandemic, undocumented workers will quietly endure illness, living in the shadows and fearing that a visit to the emergency room will lead to deportation. Looking beyond the pandemic, it is likely that the rich will continue to prosper, as they often seem to do in times of economic crisis, while the lower middle class and economically vulnerable will struggle to survive.

Studies suggest that small minority owned business will close as a result of disparities in SBA loans. Millions of Americans have been excised from the Founders' vision of liberty and justice for all, along with the goal life, liberty, and the pursuit of happiness, much of this as a result of past and present decisions of persons in power. In the richest nation in the world, poverty and lack of accessibility to health care is seldom accidental but the result of greed, structures of injustice, tax policies that benefit wealthy persons and large corporations, and acceptance of the status quo as somehow built into the nature of civic life.

Prophetic Justice-seeking.

I often challenge Christian friends who support unregulated capitalism with the assertion that the Hebraic prophets would have a moral field day with twenty-first century American economic policy. The seventh and eighth century BCE Hebraic prophets would certainly have challenged our economic priorities in this time of pandemic and beyond.[5] Inspired by their mystical encounters with the Holy One of Israel, the prophets were given unique insight into God's pain and anger at the realities of injustice. According to the prophetic troublers of Israel and their children in today's America, God hears the cries of the poor, sobs with the toddler separated from her parents, struggles with the fears of family members whose breadwinners must risk their lives to put food on our tables, and grieves with First American families experiencing higher mortality rates than other USA communities. Although their hands appear to be clean — after all they are not directly stealing or committing acts of violence, the powerful and wealthy claim — perpetrators of injustice whether in the financial sector, legal profession, temple, or politics are denounced by the Hebraic prophets because:

> They sell the righteous for silver
> and the needy for a pair of sandals -
> they who trample the head of the poor
> into the dust of the earth,
> and push the afflicted out of the way. (Amos 2:6-7)

The voice of the prophets resounds today as we look beyond pandemic. Experiencing the world through the lens of divine pathos, feeling the pain of the "fellow sufferer who understands," the prophets recognize the relationship between idolatry, immorality, and injustice. Failure to follow God's ways leads to devaluing your neighbor, seeing kin as commodities rather than God's children, and privileging profits over people.

According to the Hebraic prophets, God is passionately involved in history. The heart of the universe mourns injustice and celebrates achievement. Injustice matters not only because it deadens a child's imagination and reduces life to a matter of sheer survival but because it touches the heart of God, giving God an

---

5   I am appreciative of the ground-breaking work found in Abraham Joshua Heschel's *The Prophets* (New York: Harper Perennial, 2001) and Walter Brueggmann, *The Prophetic Imagination* (Minneapolis: Fortress Press, 2001).

ugly rather than beautiful world. God is truly, as Alfred North Whitehead claims, the fellow sufferer who understands the cries of the poor and the practices that lead to poverty and injustice,

Privileged people like myself are now experiencing a small taste of what millions of Americans experience prior to the pandemic as we jockey for paper towels and toilet paper, run out of hand sanitizer, and look fruitlessly for face masks. Lack of essential goods and services is the reality of millions every day even in the wealthiest country in the world. Lest social and theological critics like myself feel morally superior to the "cows of Bashan" in the White House, gated communities, and pandemic hideaways, we need to remember — as did the prophets — our own participation in the social evils we critique on Wall Street, banks "too big to fail," and corporations benefiting from USA tax policy. The value of many of our retirement plans has increased from the systemic injustice which benefits the bottom line of corporations in which our investments are held. We are convicted by the words of Harry Emerson Fosdick, "save us from weak resignation to the evils we deplore," as we realize our voices have been muted by our own complicity and comfort with injustice as related to our own economic wellbeing and social privilege. We are, as Thomas Merton confesses from the apparent purity of a Trappist monastery, guilty bystanders.

Although God does not cause pandemic, drought, and natural disaster, we are also weighed in the balance and facing as a society recompense for our injustice, ignorance, and apathy. Our economic and public health houses built on shifting sands have collapsed from the impact of a microscopic virus.

The Hebraic prophets saved their greatest rebuke for religious leaders and complacent temple goers — today's televangelists, and church goers defying social distancing counsel — whose praises drown out the cries of the poor and who see poverty as part of the natural economic order or as a sign of laziness, immorality, or divine disfavor.

I hate, I despise your festivals,
and I take no delight in your solemn assemblies…
Take away from me the noise of your songs;
I will not listen to the melody of your harps.
But let justice roll down like waters,
and righteousness like an ever-flowing stream.
(Amos 5:18a, 23-24)

Eight centuries later, Jesus spoke of divine judgement on the nations of the world because they neglected the hungry, thirsty, naked, and incarcerated. Recognizing that the Infinite is the Intimate, and that God feels the pain and joy of world as God's own pain and joy, Jesus announced, "as you did [did not do] unto one of the least of these, you did [did not do] to me" (Matthew 25:31-46).

Convicted by our national — and their own — neglect of the homeless, persons with mental illness, and working poor, many churches have actively responded to our society's least of these. This must become the church's new normal as we balance pastoral care within our congregation with the mandate of healing the world one person at a time.

The pandemic challenges us to new visions for our economy and justice system. The world beyond pandemic must privilege people over profits, embrace the marginalized and see their needs as trumping our largesse, provide a living wage and advance the social and economic place of those who pick, pack, and transport our food, and welcome law-abiding immigrants. Justice seeking takes us beyond our borders. Solidarity takes us beyond walls and borders to support the economic, environmental, and physical wellbeing of all God's children. In the spirit of Jewish mysticism, we must recognize that we save the world one person, neighborhood, state, and nation at a time, and that global healing must be a priority of those who follow the path of Jesus and the Hebraic prophets.

IMAGINING A JUST WORLD.

While we will "making it up as we go along" in a post-pandemic world, the quest for local and global justice requires minimally a variety of spiritual and economical initiatives such as:

- Advocacy for fair wages and health care for "essential workers" in our food and service industries.
- A humane immigration policy, including an expansion of legal services for asylum seekers, an efficient court system for immigration and asylum seekers, an end to family separation, deportation amnesty for undocumented residents who worked in "essential" food and service, health care for undocumented workers, and immediate citizenship to "dreamers" and their law-abiding parents and an efficient path to citizenship for all undocumented residents.
- The recognition that health care, housing, and voting are rights that should not be based on income, employment, neighborhood, ethnicity, and political maneuvering.
- An efficient and humane way of providing reparations for First Americans and descendants of slaves, involving communities and reservations.
- Strengthening and expanding global agencies such as the World Health Organization and calling these organizations to their highest visions.
- A national tithe from the wealthiest nations, aimed at uplifting nations in the majority world.
- Reimagining a truly global United Nations, challenging its member nations to live by the organization's vision rather than national self-interest.
- Reimagine the world banking and monetary system to benefit the poor as well as wealthy nations.
- Environmental justice including those most at risk from toxic environments, the economically vulnerable and political powerless, persons of color, as well as future generations of humans and non-humans.

The moral and spiritual arcs of history aim toward justice. Process theology's vision of God as relational and empathetic demands a creative and life-supporting transformation of our national and global structures so that all peoples may enjoy life, liberty, and the pursuit of happiness. This, I believe, is what the One who fed a multitude with five loaves and two fish, would do!

HOPEFUL ACTIVISM

During our time of the pandemic, we were told that staying on the couch was our patriotic duty. While we need to pray with our legs, as Abraham Joshua Heschel noted after marching with Martin Luther King, an active faith can be embodied in our homes and on the streets, on the phone and in the soup kitchen. Following Jesus means looking for places to share in God's quest for Shalom, embracing the local and global. There are plenty of paths toward national and global healing we can follow. Here are a few that speak to me:

- Get involved in Bread for the World, a Christian citizens movement to end hunger, calling and writing your representatives, urging them to remember the poor as they seek to reopen the economy. Remind them that when we say, "we are all in this together," we mean everyone, not just the employed, citizens, and corporations. Other groups to consider supporting are Doctors without Borders, World Vision, and your denomination's global ministries.
- Learn about the USA Poor Peoples Campaign to "save the soul of our nation." Although much of the marching will be done on social media this year, we need to respond to the reality of over 140 million caught up in poverty or economic vulnerability, much of it due to structures of social injustice and multigenerational patterns of racism, powerlessness, and poverty. As an example of the need for economic transformation, it has been reported that approximately 40% of Massachusetts families are experiencing some form of food

insecurity. I suspect that this is true of many other states in the USA.

- Consider where you need to "live simply so others can simply live" by a commitment to material, economic, and spiritual decluttering. Study the root causes of poverty, identify your complicity in injustice, and look for ways to respond creatively to hunger and poverty issues at home and abroad.

- Contact your representatives, challenging them to increase support for international organizations such as the World Health Organization and UN Human Refugee Agency. In light of the pandemic, it is clear that no nation is an island and that our national wellbeing depends on the wellbeing of other nations.

SPIRITUAL PRACTICES BEYOND THE PANDEMIC

What is a spirituality that does justice? Without justice, as Amos proclaims, we will experience a famine of hearing the world of God. When we neglect the cries of God spoken through the vulnerable, impoverished, and marginalized, we deaden our senses to God's presence.

Today, our spirituality must involve both restlessness and calm. We must experience the divine restlessness, the divine pathos, inspiring an empathetic spirituality. We also need to awaken to God's peace, breathing through us, and enabling us to become gospel people, following Jesus' vision of abundant life for all creation.

In this practice, begin with the quiet center, breathing deeply God's presence or centering our spirits through a sung prayer such as "I thank you God for the wonder of all being" or "I thank you God for the wonder of all being."

In the stillness, ask the question raised in Charles Sheldon's *In His Steps,* "Jesus, what would you have me do to be your partner in healing the world? What would you have me do in this situation? What would you have me do as I view persons in need, often caused by unjust and violent social structures — refugees, persons lining up at food banks, persons experiencing homelessness, the faces of persons experiencing malnutrition, undocumented residents in the fields?"

In light of Jesus' prayer "your kingdom come, your will be done on earth as it is in heaven," Jesus promised:

> Ask, and it will be given you; search, and you will find; knock, and the door will be opened for you. For everyone who asks receives, and everyone who searches finds, and for everyone who knocks, the door will be opened. (Acts 7:7-8)

This prayer is not a carte blanche for materialism, but a call to mission and sacrifice. When we expect great things of God, we must expect great things of ourselves, seeking to become as much like Jesus as possible through compassionate action. God promises that if we ask to follow the way of Jesus, he will show us the way in the spirit of social gospel pastor Washington Gladdon's hymn:

> O Master, let me walk with Thee,
> In lowly paths of service free;
> Tell me Thy secret; help me bear
> The strain of toil, the fret of care.
>
> Help me the slow of heart to move
> By some clear, winning word of love;
> Teach me the wayward feet to stay,
> And guide them in the homeward way.
>
> Teach me Thy patience; still with Thee
> In closer, dearer, company,
> In work that keeps faith sweet and strong,
> In trust that triumphs over wrong.
>
> In hope that sends a shining ray
> Far down the future's broad'ning way,
> In peace that only Thou canst give,
> With Thee, O Master, let me live.

PRAYING FOR HEALING IN A TIME OF PANDEMIC

*Let me walk with you, Loving Companion. Let me feel your
pain and joy. Let your senses be mine. Let me move from apathy to
empathy and passivity to prophetic passion. Let me be your companion in healing the world. Amen.*

CHAPTER SIX

PROPHETIC HEALING

When Israel was a child, I loved him,
and out of Egypt I called my son.
The more called them,
the more they went from me;
they kept sacrificing to the Baals,
and offering incense to idols…

How can I give you up, Ephraim?
How can I hand you over, O Israel?...
My heart recoils within me;
my compassion grows warm and tender.
I will not execute my fierce anger;
I will not again destroy Ephraim;
for I am God and no mortal,
the Holy One in your midst,
and I will not come in wrath. (Hosea 11:1-2, 8a, 9)

The times cry out for prophetic hopefulness. Our national and global priorities have rested on the shifting sands of injustice, consumption, nationalism, and environmental destruction. Many of our religious leaders have conflated God and country and more diabolically God and political leadership, defying science and scripture to shore up hoped-for political and judicial power. The prophetic word recognizes the signs of the times. While prophetic protest, reflecting God's vision of Shalom, is not punitive, it recognizes that acts have consequences. Injustice, income inequality, and neglect of the vulnerable leads to social upheaval. Prophets then and now proclaim an alternative vision to the values that have contributed to their nation's current crisis, whether in the 8th century BCE or 21st century United States and the Western world. In words initially coined by author and humorist Finley Peter Dunne to describe the vocation of the press, prophets are called to "comfort the afflicted, and afflict the comfortable."

Comfort and critique are essential to the quest for justice and the embodiment of God's vision for the powerless and powerful alike. Prophets then and now confess, in the words of Theodore Parker, that they "do not pretend to understand the moral universe, the arc is a long one," but they are certain that the arc of the universe "bends toward justice." The moral and spiritual arc inspire prophetic restlessness and challenge, they also inspire the quest for prophetic healing the embraces the planet in its entirety, reconciling enemies and promoting unity amid diversity.

HEALING AND PROTEST

The times cry out for prophetic critique. But, within the critique is the quest for healing, grounded in the prophet's hope for personal and cultural conversion. God has a stake in the historical process and God's moral and spiritual arc is moving through the world and each nation, inspiring visions of justice and healing. While the quest for justice is often adversarial, with winners and losers, conflict cannot be the final word if the nation is to "let justice roll down like waters and righteousness like an ever-flowing stream." Amid the prophetic challenge is the hope for prophetic healing beyond conflict and opposition.

Prophetic healing involves our commitment to challenge the injustice while recognizing God's presence in ourselves and in those with whom we contend in the political and social arenas. Prophetic healing is grounded in the belief that we are truly all in this together. Saint and sinner, rich and poor, conservative and progressive, powerful and powerless, and oppressor and oppressed, are joined in God's beloved community. The prophetic healer recognizes that healing must embrace all of us if it is to be lasting for any of us. All of us need of grace and healing. All of us bear the imprint of God's loving creativity, at work even in the most recalcitrant individualist or self-interested politician.

Prophet healers speak truth to power, confronting those who perpetrate injustice and destruction in the human and non-human worlds. Yet, like surgeons, their interventions are intended to cure rather than destroy. Our quest as God's healing agents is to transcend polarization and alienation to experience the common identity we all share as God's children, despite profound differences in ethics and public policy. Strong words may be uttered and profound change is necessary in the quest for justice but our goal is to achieve social transformation by embodying non-violent and reconciling responses toward those whose views practices we oppose, without engaging in divisive power plays ourselves. Prophetic healing seeks a pathway of social and political wholeness that binds together diverse communities, rich and poor, male and female, citizen and immigrant, left and right, and atheist and believer.

In describing his own prophetic mysticism, one of my mentors, African American theologian and pastor Howard Thurman, asserts that the mystic, inspired by the encounter with God, "seek[s] to remove anything that prevents the individual from free and easy access to his own altar-stair that is in his own heart."[6] Capitalist and socialist, wealthy and poor, are all in need of God's healing touch. Those of us who protest injustice must confess our own complicity in structures of injustice. Our recognition that we also benefit from economic inequity and environmental destruction prevents us from polarization and moral superiority, in which we — like the biblical literalist — build walls between the saved and unsaved, and just and unjust. Our quest for justice must reflect Jesus' recognition that God makes "the sun rise on the evil and the good, and sends rain on the unrighteous and the righteous" (Matthew 5:45).

Our personal and social salvation requires some to sacrifice and others to protest, some to simplify and others to acquire. Our

---

6   Howard Thurman, *Mysticism and Social Action: Lawrence Lectures and Discussions with Dr. Howard Thurman* (London: International Association for Religious Freedom, 2014), Kindle location, 270-274.

spiritual lives are at stake in the quest for prophetic healing and conciliatory justice. Hatred deadens the spirits of protesters. Poverty diminishes the imagination of children. Apathy hardens the hearts of the wealthy. Injustice destroys the souls of the powerful. As impossible as it may seem, the quest for healing must encompass all of us if we are to be part of God's Shalom beyond pandemic.

The cries of injustice, the protests of poverty, must be heard and the wealthy and powerful must recognize the "blind side" that has mired them in apathy and drowned out God's voice despite the opulence of their megachurches and sophistication of their praise bands. The wealthy and powerful are called to lamentations of regret for their insensitivity and confessions of guilt for the pain they knowingly and unknowingly caused. We who consider ourselves middle class may also be challenged to lament the contrast between our privilege and others' poverty. Our spiritual healing depends on significant sacrifices in terms of possession and power so millions can have educational, housing, dietary, medical, and economic essentials, This time of pandemic may be "day of salvation" if we trust God's moral and spiritual arc enough to embrace justice, hospitality, and Shalom in relationship to "friend" and "foe" alike.

HOPEFUL ACTIVISM

Words matter, sometimes almost as much as actions. Words can diminish, destroy, damage, and denigrate. Words can affirm and alienation. As I write these words in late April 2020, Donald Trump has disavowed any responsibility for the emergency calls to hotlines and hospitals following his suggestion that injecting disinfectant might be effective in treating the Coronavirus. To him and many other politicians and their followers, any form of confession or responsibility-taken is a sign of weakness. In contrast, taking responsibility and confession for shortcomings is a sign of spiritual strength and maturity and can be the first step to healing personal and societal wounds. Beyond that, words of welcome, affirmation, and encouragement deepen relationships and transform spirits.

Jesus, John the Baptist, and the Hebraic prophets challenged injustice, religious vacuity and legalism, and self-righteousness with harsh words at times. No one wants to be called a "cow of Bashan," "white washed tomb," or "brood of vipers," though at certain times the shoe fits. While we may not resort to such graphic language, there are times when we insult others, in contrast to Jesus and the prophets, with no redemptive purpose. We simply want to demolish another's position or show them for the fool they are for supporting a particular social or political policy or politician. We see evidence of this regularly on social media, where I have been called all manner of expletives from people I barely know. While I am not without sin, I have made it my policy to communicate with a sense of grace even when I challenge another's behavior or opinion. I believe that social media can be sacramental and even redemptive when we speak our truth with love and seek to built bridges rather than walls.[7]

Hopeful activism involves seeing the divine in your opponents and translating your vision into forceful but caring comments. Take time to examine your comments to those with whom you disagree both on social media and in person. Do you seek to speak the truth with love? Do you look for common ground? Do you challenge positions without denigrating them personally?

There will be a good deal of finger pointing and critique in the post-pandemic world. Recognition of culpability and righting socially and politically inflicted injustice is necessary if we are to move toward God's realm of Shalom and dismantle the structures of injustice and ecological destruction. But, along with deconstruction must come the creative healing that is essential for there to be reconciliation and respect, even when we differ. We can live with diversity without resorting to polarization.

---

7   For more on the spirituality of social media, see Bruce Epperly *God Online: A Mystic's Guide to the Internet* (Vestal, NY: Anamchara Books, 2020).

SPIRITUALITY BEYOND PANDEMIC

My grandsons and I have laughed long and loud at the film "Despicable Me," which describes Felonious Gru's transformation from arch-villain to loving caregiver. Like many other happy ending stories, such as Charles Dickens' *A Christmas Carol,* "Despicable Me," reveals the goodness hidden beneath an unattractive exterior. I must admit that on occasion I use words like "despicable" and "diabolical" to describe certain political leaders, who from my perspective appear driven only by ego, self-interest, and political gain. It is difficult for me to imagine any goodness within them. Yet, as Luke Skywalker discovers, there is even some goodness left in Darth Vader, and his affirmation of Vader's goodness brings out the diabolical leader's parental love.

In this spiritual practice, I invite you to identify your villains. Who is public enemy number one for you? It might be a president or political leader, a corporate CEO, a cluster of protesters wanting to reopen America, crowds chanting at a political rally, or cable television political commentators. After identifying your villains, take a few moments to breathe deeply, refocusing your attention to see something, perhaps deep down, holy about them, something of which they may not be aware. Within those adults you find despicable, see the frightened or emotionally abused child, the insecure adult needing constant adulation, the emotionally immature political leader boasting of his prowess and fearing neglect. Recognizing your own imperfections and struggles, pray that those for whom you pray might find peace, a sense of wholeness, and experience transformation in accordance with God's vision not necessarily your own. Pray that they — and you — might follow the better angels of their nature as you remember two more verses from the revival hymn:

> Just as I am — Thou wilt receive,
> Wilt welcome, pardon, cleanse, relieve;
> Because Thy promise I believe,
> — O Lamb of God, I come!

Just as I am — Thy love unknown
Has broken every barrier down;
Now to be Thine, yea, Thine alone,
— O Lamb of God, I come!

Praying for Healing in a Time of Pandemic

Holy One, help me to challenge and love, to see the holiness of those I am tempted to condemn. To seek justice while caring for the souls of oppressors. Let me recognize my own sin and brokenness, feeling solidarity with those whose practices and views I oppose, recognizing we are both God's children in need of healing grace. Amen.

CHAPTER SEVEN

PEACE

Jesus said to them again, "Peace be with you. As the Father has sent me, so I send you." When he had said this, he breathed on them and said to them, "Receive the Holy Spirit." (John 20:21-22)

Sheltering in place, fearful of the religious and political authorities, Jesus' first followers encounter the Risen One, who breathes on them, filling them with the peace that passes all understanding and giving them the courage and voice to proclaim the good news that death has been defeated, the world has changed, for "Christ is alive." The peace that God gives emerges in times of threat and tragedy. It embraces our pain, yet sees within our personal, national, and global trauma, seeds of hope for the incarnation of God's new earth.

In contrast, court preachers, according to the Hebraic prophets, echo the king's triumphant message, proclaim "peace, peace, when there is no peace." The peace they promote denies the reality of political upheaval, poverty, and plague. Peace means going back to the way things were, preserving the threatened status quo, and advocating the binary world of insiders and outsiders in the economy and God's realm. Court preachers, then and now, advocate a religious exceptionalism, mirroring nation-first exceptionalism, as they assure their followers that their faith will immunize them against plague and Coronavirus, despite their refusal to practice safe physical distancing. Their proclamation of peace is reflected in the "right" of Christians to worship when and where they please without consequences or responsibility for the health of their neighbors. Presuming themselves faithful or looking for a talisman to protect them, they disregard those outside their circle of faith, whose apparent lack of faith puts them at greater risk from the divine judgment visited through COVID-19. While strong on piety, these pastors and their followers are weak on responsibility and compassion to those outside their circle. They may even be weak on faith as they limit divine revelation to their sanctuaries and way of life. Lacking trust in God's future, they seek to deny or minimize dangers in the present pandemic, fearing the impact of the pandemic on their promises of prosperity for the faithful.

PEACE AS LOCAL AND GLOBAL

I believe that peace involves much more than individualistic witnesses to faith. Peace takes us beyond self-interest or spiritual superiority to solidarity with all creation. Peace is grounded in the interplay of God's providential care and challenge and our faithful and sacrificial responsiveness. God is at work in each moment of experience. As Whitehead observes, God's "purpose is always embodied in particular ideals relevant to the actual state of the world… Every act leaves the world with a deeper or fainter impress of God. He then passes to his next relation to the world with enlarged, or diminished, presentation of ideal values."[8] Life is a call and response in which we neither passive victims nor apathetic observers but active companions and partners in God's realm of Shalom. What we do shapes the intensity of God's presence and power in the world. Peace comes for recognizing that we are part of a holy adventure, in which we are invited see our personal and national adventures as part of a larger planetary and cosmic adventure.

Peace emerges when we claim our place in the intricate, interdependent, and evolving "body of Christ," whose reality ranges far beyond church or Christianity but embraces the good earth and the enveloping universe. The moral and spiritual arc of history runs through our nation and our churches, but also takes shape in the global community and non-human world. Claiming our identity as world citizens, we discover that peace comes when we trust that

8   Alfred North Whitehead, *Religion in the Making (New York: Meridian Books, 1972),* 152.

what we do matters, shapes God's experience, and is treasured forever in God's memory.

Each moment evokes a decision — will we add to the beauty or ugliness of the world? Will be life-givers or death-dealers? The path of peace involves ever-widening spirals of compassion, moving us from self-interest to world loyalty. Following the path of Jesus, we can choose to "lose" our lives, the life of self-concern and individualism and success obtained at the expense of the weak and marginalized, to "gain" our lives as part of God's holy adventure. In the words of Whitehead, "Peace is self-control at its widest, — at the 'width' where the self has been lost and interest has been transferred to coordinations wider than personality."[9]

PRACTICING PEACE.

At first glance, my reflections on peace may seem mired in theological abstraction, unrelated to the day to day anxieties most of us feel. Yet, theology matters. Our vision of God and the world, and our role in shaping the world, can be a matter of life and death for ourselves and our cities, nation, and planet. A binary God, all-powerfully determining and judging the planet, encourages binary or dualistic self-interest and separates people of faith from faithless unbelievers. The binary judge, punishing the infidel and immoral with plague and virus encourages moral and spiritual complacency and the politics of domination. Believing ourselves to be chosen, we believe that we deserve our prosperity and health, while others' poverty and disease is equally deserved either as result of divine justice or decision-making. While I do not doubt the sincerity of those who follow the judging, all-powerful God, a sense of individualistic self-interest permeates their piety. Their peace is bought at the price of neglecting others' suffering in this world and the next. With heaven as their destination, salvation becomes a matter of individualistic belief. Following the sovereign God and his emissaries in the political arena, this individualistic piety has

9   Alfred North Whitehead, *Adventures in Ideas* (New York: Free Press, 1961), 285.

tragically led to baptizing self-interest in economics and foreign policy as God's way in the world. It has encouraged complacency about addressing social injustice and climate change, based on the assumption that salvation is primarily individual and has little to do with social and economic structures.

In contrast, relational visions of God promote social responsibility, politics of compassion and inclusion, openness to diversity, and balance national self-affirmation with global responsibility. God is with us — all of us — and encourages us to embrace one another, across national, ethnic, religious, and economic differences. Open to the universe, our adventures are part of a greater adventure, inviting us to greater and more inclusive personal and community stature. Once again, let me quote Whitehead, "Peace is self-control at its widest, — at the 'width' where the self has been lost and interest has been transferred to co-ordinations wider than personality."[10] Peace takes us beyond individualism to planetary citizenship. While heaven may be our destination, we can experience heaven in the here and now if we live according to God's vision of Shalom and its embrace of all creation.

In the wake of pandemic — or dare we say, in this ongoing pandemic and other future crises such as climate change for which we are equally unprepared — world loyalty invites us to global hospitality and compassion, in which our neighbor person and neighbor land is anyone in need. Like the Good Samaritan of Jesus' parable, we cross boundaries to be part of God's healing process. There is no "other" as we identify our wellbeing with that of others. The path of peace takes us beyond our privilege to imagining sacrificial living and social transformation that may not always be to our economic or political advantage. But, beyond the sacrifice is joy and the peace emerging from companionship with God and all God's children.

---

10   Alfred North Whitehead, *Adventures in Ideas,* 285.

HOPEFUL ACTIVISM

Hopeful living in times of crisis involves the recognition that God is a circle whose center is everywhere and whose circumference is nowhere. God's center is right where I am and that requires me to care for my family and myself, to honor and cherish God's presence in my immediate circle of care. During the pandemic, I wear a mask whenever I walk on the Cape Cod beaches as a witness to my care for others as well as my vocation to care for myself so that I might fulfill my roles as grandparent, pastor, writer, and citizen. Yet, the center is everywhere. God is in all things, and I must honor God's presence in the "other" by promoting their wellbeing so that they might also experience abundant life.

In a God-filled world, justice-seeking means the joining of individual and global acts of compassion. It means letting go of my largesse to ensure that, in my immediate environment, people have the basics necessary for survival and to provide housing, education, and health care for their families. This involves the willingness to generously contribute financially to causes greater than myself, locally to food pantries and homeless shelters and globally to organizations providing food and medical care in other nations. It also means the willingness to sacrifice power and privilege through advocating politically for changes that help others determine their economic and political destinies in a compassionate, democratic society. Peace means sacrificing — living simply and promoting policies of simplicity — so that others may live. It means, as I suggested in the chapter on prophetic healing, that I commit myself to acts of reconciliation to counter the incivility and alienation promoted in politics and social media. Even for prudent Good Samaritans, who — like myself — have homes and retirement plans, God's call is to see our joy and sorrow connected to that of others, and love our neighbors as ourselves by working toward their wellbeing in personal interactions and social structures that promote beauty and justice

Spirituality In the Time of Pandemic

The peace we yearn for begins with us. Peace unites inner and out, and contemplation and activism. Once more begin with breathing, experiencing God's enlivening and enlightening energy in your cells and your soul. Experience God's breath entering you as a healing light, reflecting your own chosen healing color — green, white, yellow, blue, purple, and so forth. Let the light heal of God your spirit. Once you feel a sense of personal centeredness, experience the breath you exhale as a healing light permeating the world, beginning with yourself, home and neighborhood, community, state, nation, earth, and beyond. Feel your healing unity with all creation in ever wider circles of compassion. Then, let the light return from the far horizon to your personal life, filling you and all creation with God's healing love.

Praying for Healing in a Time of Pandemic.

Let there be peace on earth. Let your peace, Living and Loving God, begin in and with me. May I be an instrument of peace, bringing peace to all I meet and to this good earth. Amen.

CHAPTER EIGHT

HOPE — CHURCH BEYOND PANDEMIC

For thus says the LORD: Only when Babylon's seventy years are completed will I visit you, and I will fulfill to you my promise and bring you back to this place. For surely I know the plans I have for you, says the LORD, plans for your welfare and not for harm, to give you a future with hope. Then when you call upon me and come and pray to me, I will hear you. When you search for me, you will find me; if you seek me with all your heart, I will let you find me, says the Lord, and I will restore your fortunes and gather you from all the nations and all the places where I have driven you, says the Lord, and I will bring you back to the place from which I sent you into exile. (Jeremiah 29:11-14)

I am a pastor in process and I pastor a church in process. The pandemic has challenged many of my assumptions about our nation's economy and values. It has also called into question how I will do ministry and how we will do church beyond pandemic. On a lovely afternoon in early March, I was planning for the Easter sunrise service on Craigville Beach, a celebrative service in the sanctuary, and a brunch and egg hunt after church. None of that came to pass. On Easter morning, in a different world, we gathered on Zoom and made, to be generous, a beautiful noise singing "Christ the Lord is Risen Today!" Like many I did not imagine holding worship services, adult faith formation classes, and daily prayer online. Nor did I imagine driving past our shuttered church, seeing our marque message proclaiming "This Sunday Our Doors May be Closed, But God's Heart is Open." I have wrestled with budget concerns during the pandemic and I have grieved my inability to visit shut-ins, hospitalized members, and lead memorial services and gravesides. As we plan for the reopening of church, we are filled with uncertainty and indecision. Like other church leaders, we are asking questions such as: When will we reopen? What will we do about traditional staples of church life — the passing of the peace, congregational singing, communion, fellowship time following worship, children's faith formation, church potlucks, and community events such as the Memorial Day Parade, our congregation's vendor faire and lobster roll supper? We wonder if we will be reduced to bowing with "namaste" or fist or elbow bumps during the passing of the peace or forgoing the Peace except in our hearts (and not our hands) during worship? Is the pastor's receiving line following worship a thing of the past? More importantly, what will church itself be like — theologically, missionally, pastorally, and politically in the future?

You may notice that I haven't used the term "the church" in this text. I have come to realize more fully than ever during the pandemic that God's presence is universal, revelation is constant and ubiquitous, and that the sacred is secular, embodied in everyday life. In contrast to the sacred, church bodies can tragically betray their vocation and enthrone secular — economic, individualistic, nationalistic and power-centered — values as reflective of God's vision. I use the humble terms "church" and "churches" as a recognition that church as institution — along with priesthood, ministry, and spiritual leadership — does not enjoy a unique metaphysical status.

In fact, seeing church as unique may be the greatest detriment to its ministry moving forward. If, as I believe, God reveals truth and beauty in all things, human and non-human, church's uniqueness lies not in its metaphysical separation from the "world" but in its intentionality — its desire to follow the way of Jesus, look for holiness in all people and places, and seek to do something beautiful for God. While this intentionality may appear different in "kind" and often sets church in contrast to the world, especially when it follows the paths of compassion, healing, reconciliation, and prophetic witness, a faithful church recognizes that God can inspire persons beyond its doors to do God's world-transforming work. Moreover, faithful church leaders and congregants need to remember that church shares in the ambiguity of every institution, even when it is at its best: churches desire to preserve their physical witness, often their brick and mortar, as they go out into the world sacrificially. Churches have inspired charity and inclusion, they have also been agents of persecution, alienation, and violence. As we move beyond pandemic, and face new crises, we must heed the words of the apostle Paul: "Do not be conformed to this world, but be transformed by the renewing of your minds so that you can discern the will of God — what is good and acceptable and perfect" (Romans 12:2).

It is my practice on my sunrise beach walk to pray for the congregation I pastor, South Congregational Church, United Church of Christ, when I see the church steeple peeking out from the trees on a bluff about Craigville Beach, here in Centerville, Massachusetts. This morning the steeple was shrouded in mist. Although I could not see the steeple's outline, I knew that it was there, albeit hidden, as a call to prayer for church and people. My experience reflects my feelings about church today, not only the congregation I pastor today from my home, and online, but church mission in a post-pandemic world when we hopefully return to our sanctuary for public worship. The future is uncertain and shrouded in uncertainly. We can barely see our way forward but we must prayerfully take one step at a time, aligning ourselves as fully as we can with the moral and spiritual arc of history.

When I returned home from my beach walk, I was presented with another spiritual message, this time painted on my coffee cup, "For surely I know the plans I have for you, says the Lord, plans for your welfare and not for harm, to give you a future with hope" (Jeremiah 29:11). When Jeremiah heard these words, resonating in his spirit, he was no more certain about the future of the nation and its houses of worship than we are today. His nation was in shambles and worship in disarray. The people had turned from God and were experiencing the consequences of their idolatry and injustice. Yet, Jeremiah experienced a deeper reality within and beyond tragedy. God's vision was at work, giving shape to the future and illuminating the tentative steps of those who turned to God for guidance.

Everyone from newscasters, celebrities sheltering in place, neighbors and people I meet in passing on the beach, as well as scientists and politicians, chant "we'll great through this." I believe they are right, although everyone knows that our churches, personal lives, and nation — like a person recovering from a life-threatening illness — will be changed forever. We can't go back. Nor should church every go back. Treasuring past achievements, God always guides us toward the far horizon, guiding us one step at a time. We cannot be conformed to old ways, as vital as they were, but must transform what is best as we lean toward the future emerging in this time of pandemic. In fact, we may never reopen church as it once was. Some commentators say that the days of Las Vegas casinos, dinner and a movie, airline travel, and mass athletic events are over or will be radically different, at least for the foreseeable future. This same reality may affect churches, especially those with older members, whose churchgoing may be perceived as a matter of life and death. Megachurches and their opulent pastoral staffs may become the victim of peoples' desire for safe, distant seating. Zoom services may complement public worship for churches who did not life stream their services before the pandemic.

Claiming no expertise at discerning the future either spiritually or scientifically, I once again turned to my Facebook friends, for wisdom and guidance related to their hopes, fears, and dreams for church beyond pandemic. Their responses were illuminating. Most of my respondents feared that the church would go back to life as usual, and things will pick up quickly in terms of budget and attendance. One respondent noted, "Things will never be the same again, and we must move forward. A lot of churches will have to scale down their programs and staff. Others will simply close for lack of attendance and income." Another expressed the fear that "churches will no longer afford their buildings" and then expressed the hope that "church will realize that its mission has never been restricted to the sanctuary but is out in the world."

Looking toward the future, many see the Coronavirus as the invitation to explore a new kind of church. They recognize that sanctuaries and traditions are important, but they also imagine a different kind of church, initiating novelty to match the novelties of the era of pandemic:

— Church needs to live out the Sermon on the Mount and be a place that blesses those who struggle to make ends meet, mourn the loss of friends and family, and live with insecurity. The Beatitudes must guide our way forward.
— Church is called to be a place of community, on the move, and making it up as it goes along in terms of worship and ministry.
— Church needs to see the sanctuary as a springboard to service.
— Social media and online worship need to continue especially for persons with disabilities.
— Church is called to prepare and prevent the next crisis, global climate change.
— Mission must come first, building second.
— Healing of body, mind, spirit, and society must be from and center for post-pandemic church.

All of my respondents affirm the lure of old ways of doing church. They appreciate the hymns, sanctuaries, potluck suppers, and congregational traditions; they also imagine a lively, agile church, emphasizing high touch technologies, encouraging small group ministries, and seeing mission as encompassing every aspect of church life.

God invites us to see a way forward when previously we saw no future ahead. In partnership with people of good will of all perspectives and religious traditions, church beyond sanctuary is called to make the whole world a sanctuary — a holy place for holy people, claiming its vocation as an agent sharing in God's vision of healing the earth.

HOPEFUL ACTIVISM

Virtually all of scripture was written in times of personal and national challenge. One need only think of the book of Job, born out of the universal experience of unjust suffering; the prophets condemning injustice and then providing a glimmer of hope for a people in exile; the book of Ruth, describing famine, economic destitution, bereavement, and the challenge of racism toward foreign brides; the crucifixion of Jesus; and the persecution of Jesus' first followers.

In our own time of crisis, we need to visualize hopeful futures, born of realistic observation, not magical thinking and denial. What futures do you imagine for your congregation? In what way do you visualize your congregation moving forward in terms of mission, finances, worship, spiritual growth, and mission to the community? In response to these visions, what first steps can you encourage your congregation to take as it embraces a challenging and hopeful future?

SPIRITUALITY IN A TIME OF PANDEMIC

The pandemic surfaced as our congregation was in the process of beginning planning for its 225th anniversary. In the course of its 224 year history, our congregation has responded to a variety of "impossibilities" — planting a church in a village to respond to the moral and spiritual needs of the neighborhood, moving the original sanctuary piece by piece by horse drawn wagons to a new location, choosing to become an abolitionist congregation, and then living through the Civil War, Spanish Flu in 1918, the Great Depression, and various controversies leading to pastoral departures and membership losses. We are survivors, and now our survival depends on deepening our faith and out of deep faith, reaching out in mission. Our parents in the faith did not fully know where they were going, and neither do we.

Not knowing the future or the right course for our congregations, let us focus on a simple prayer — to constantly ask for God's guidance. Let us pray, "Grant us wisdom for path ahead. Show us the way and give us courage to be faithful. Help us find God's path of salvation for our time and place." Then let us listen for God's voice in our personal and corporate life as we explore new ways of being church with hope beyond pandemic. With Harry Emerson Fosdick, let us ask God to:

> Grant us wisdom
> Grant us courage
> For the living of these days.

PRAYING FOR HEALING IN A TIME OF PANDEMIC.

Awaken us to possibility hidden in tragedy. Hope hidden in despair. Life bursting forth from death. Enliven and enlighten us that we might live out your mission in this challenging time. Amen.

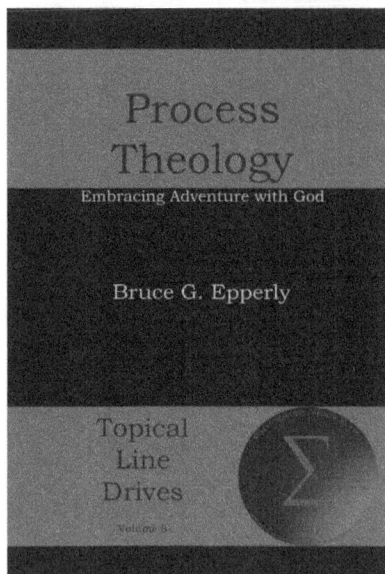

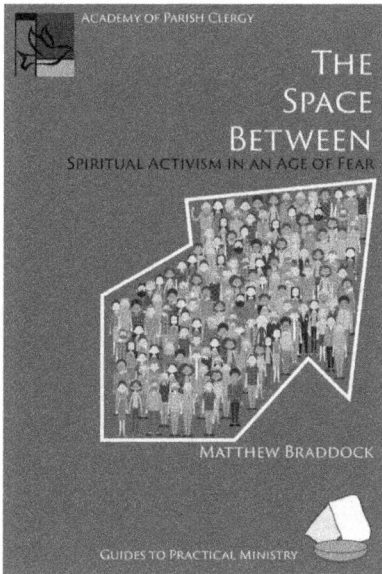

The Space Between will help you construct a reflective search for the loving justice of a living God.

Grace Ji-Sun Kim,
Associate Professor of Theology
at Earlham School of Religion

Through the storm,
A whisper.
Through the night,
A shaft of light.
Lingering there in the heavy
air,
A promise.
This is not the end.
A beginning dancing,
Just out of sight.

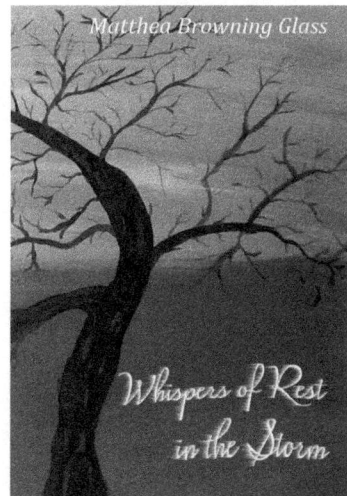

Matthea Browning Glass

Whispers of Rest
in the Storm